Brunch with an Irish flavour

Brunch with an Irish flavour

Alacoque Meehan

A. & A. Farmar

First published in 1999 by

A. & A. Farmar

Beech House, 78 Ranelagh Village

Dublin 6, Ireland

Tel + 353 1 496 3625 Fax + 353 1 497 0107

Email: afarmar@iol.ie

ISBN 1-899047-53-0

The drawings on pp 9, 10, 38, 43, 46, 61, 76, 117 and 124
are by Pauline O'Reilly; the rest are by Jacques Teljeur.

To Anne and Ken

Aknowledgements

I wish to thank my parents Anne and Ken Meehan for their love and support.

I thank my siblings Deborah Veale, Ruth Meehan, Kenneth Meehan and particularly Alex Meehan who helped me enormously. Thanks to my extended family Sorcha Veale, Charlie Hanrahan and Jeannette Doyle.

Thanks to Kevin Burke for access to his library.

Thanks to Caroline McCormac for some American inspiration.

Thanks to Dave Gallagher for his expert opinion.

Thanks to my great friends Orla Murphy, Kathleen Mc Mahon and Sara Burke and indeed all the rest of my friends who have helped me to prepare, to serve, to eat and drink, to practice and perfect *Brunch with an Irish Flavour*.

Alacoque Meehan

June 1999

Contents

Part 2 Drinking

Introduction

Although American in origin, brunch is a meal that suits the Irish temperament. A little more effort than breakfast but a lot less than lunch, it's a relaxed social occasion where you can unwind with your friends, have a drink or two and catch up on the weekend gossip.

As a nation we are renowned for our willingness, at the drop of a hang-over, to get together around a table of a weekend. For this reason I chose to dedicate a book completely to the subject of 'Brunch with an Irish Flavour'.

Armed with this book, even the most culinarily challenged amongst us can throw a damned good brunch party and entertain with flair.

Before you start

Check the **ingredients** list—there is nothing more infuriating than getting half-way through a recipe only to find that a crucial item is missing from the store-cupboard. The ingredients list also describes how the inputs should be prepared (chopped, thinly sliced, into cubes etc.).

Next read the whole recipe to get a sense of how long the dish will take (i.e. whether you should have started yesterday), and what equipment you'll need. Then begin.

All recipes have **metric, imperial** and **American** measures but you should stick to one set, since the conversions cannot be exact (e.g. 8 oz is strictly equal to 226.8 g, a quantity that would defeat most kitchen scales). So the proportions are worked out separately in each measure.

Cooking **times and temperatures** vary from oven to oven and measures vary from scales to scales, so the times and measures I have given are guidelines only. Use your common sense, especially when adding flavourings or garnishes and checking cooking times, to judge what tastes and looks just right, when food is cooked and dishes are ready. Whatever you cook is ready when it looks and tastes good so it's very important to taste continually when you are cooking.

Be proud and confident when you present your guests with a dish you have prepared. If you tell them that it's delicious, unless it's an inedible mess, they'll believe you.

When you're giving a brunch party don't get stressed out before your guests arrive. As long as you have prepared in advance you'll be fine, so **make lists**.

Make a list of your guests, make a list of what you are going to cook, make a shopping list, make a list of what you can prepare in advance. Make a timed list of preparations to be done in advance so that you can see at a glance what you have to do; for example:

> **sausages can be made the day before**
>
> **bread should be made the morning of the brunch party**

white wine and champagne need to be chilled two hours before the guests arrive

hollandaise sauce needs to be made not more than an hour before serving

oysters need to be opened just before eating.

Write a list like this:

Make sausages	Saturday
Make bread	Sunday 9 a.m.
Chill wine	Sunday 11 a.m.
Make hollandaise	Sunday 1 p. m.
Open oysters	Sunday 1.15 p.m.

If you write down everything you have to do like this you can cross things off as you do them. This makes me feel very organised. On the other hand, writing a list like this this is supposed to help you, not scare you. If you don't manage to get things done in time don't worry, enlist one of your guests to help. The worst thing that can happen is that people will have to wait a little longer and drink a little more before eating which will whet their appetite and and so they will enjoy the food even more.

It is worth remembering not to drink too much yourself before you are ready to sit down because unless you are proficient at cooking while drunk (in which case you are probably a top chef already) it can ruin all your efforts. An incapacitated host is rarely a pretty sight.

Drinks

Having said that, drinks are a very important part of a brunch party and you should always provide the best you can afford from what's available.

You should serve tea, coffee, fruit juice and chilled white wine or a light red at room temperature. Anything else is a delicious extravagance but it is always fun to have a cocktail or two.

Once you have the right ingredients coffee-making is something that can be successfully delegated along with tea-making, orange-squeezing, cocktail-shaking and indeed, bottle-opening. Allow half to three-quarters of a bottle of wine per person and a quarter bottle of mineral water per person.

If you are making cocktails you could ask close friends to bring one of the ingredients such as Galliano or Grenadine.

Suggested menus

In creating a menu, variety is the spice of life. Try to include dishes from each of the chapters, so as to suit all tastes and ages. Most of the dishes are suitable for vegetarians. On the other hand, hardened carnivores need more than eggs and brioche to keep them cheerful. Fruit will make you feel virtuous first thing in the morning and sugary sweet things will restore your sugar balance if it has been depleted from the night before.

Money no object

If you're not counting the cost I suggest you serve the following dishes and drinks together:

Bellinis, coffee and fruit juice

Iced shellfish platter

Lobster Newburg

Spinach cocottes and freshly baked baguette

Blinis with caviar and sour cream

Brioche with lemon curd; banana hotcakes

Vintage champagne throughout

(If money is really no object, give this book to someone else and pay them to prepare brunch for you.)

Feeding the five thousand

For entertaining a large group on a restricted budget here is a delicious, inexpensive menu:

Mimosa, made with a sparkling wine such as cava

Kedgeree

Devilled kidneys

Potato farls

French toast

Iced fruit platter

The following recipes lend themselves to buffet style presentation.

Large pitchers of Bloody Mary

Tortilla Espagnole served cold and cut into wedges

Focaccia

Brown soda bread

Cajun prawns

Lobster, green bean and new potato salad

Iced shellfish platter

Pork and chorizo sausages

Hash browns

Chocolate and walnut muffins

Pineapple and banana kebabs

Show-off specials

If you are quite good at cooking here are a few of the slightly more complicated recipes:

Eggs Benedict

Crab cakes with chilli mayonnaise

Lobster Newburg

Freshly made baguette

Brioche

Croissants with lemon curd

Home-made yoghurt with honey

Klutz corner

If you are not so good at cooking but still want to have a go here is a menu that you can prepare with minimum effort:

Heuvos rancheros: buy flour tortillas and spicy salsa, fry some eggs, and serve together with some sliced avocado.

Oysters: ask your fishmonger to open them for you and serve on a bed of ice shortly afterwards.

Cheeseboard: buy a selection of ripe cheese and serve with some good fresh bread.

Welsh rarebit: after all it's just fancy cheese on toast.

Iced fruit platter: couldn't be easier.

Don't forget that a little presentation goes a long way, so dig out or borrow some really nice serving plates and dishes and have plenty of fresh herbs, sliced lemon etc. on hand to decorate the dishes.

Keeping the kids happy

As most brunch parties are held at the weekend the presence of children is inevitable so here is a menu suitable for all ages.

UFO eggs

Beignets—you can tell kids they're doughnuts

Fish cakes

Pork sausages—you can make these cocktail size

Hash browns

Banana hotcakes

Fresh fruit shake.

A few tips

If you find **anchovies** too salty simply soak them in milk for half an hour before using

When cooking **bacon** for a brunch party, bake it on racks in the oven as this saves time and space. Bacon is delicious when brushed with a little honey before cooking.

Descaling **fish** will be a lot easier if you first briefly pour boiling water over it.

Store peeled cloves of **garlic** under a layer of olive oil. This preserves them and you can also use the oil for dressings and sauces.

The best way to peel a clove of garlic is to lightly crush it under the flat blade of your chopping knife. The skin will break and slip off easily.

When crushing peeled garlic to a paste with a chopping knife, add a pinch of salt. This helps to break up the garlic and also absorbs the juice so you get all the flavour. Remember to correct for seasoning accordingly in whatever dish you are preparing.

It is nearly impossible to remove the smell of garlic or onions from your hands after cooking. Wash well with detergent and lemon juice and live with it!

Preserve fresh **ginger** in a jar of vodka.

Soaking **kippers** in hot water for a short time before grilling (broiling) will make them less oily and less dry.

Before squeezing **lemons, limes and oranges** heat them for a few seconds in the microwave—you will get more juice from them.

To wash **lettuce** for a large number of people, you should first fill your sink with cold salted water then add the trimmed lettuce, separated into leaves. Let it soak there for a few minutes then remove the leaves and empty the sink. Repeat the process. Remove the lettuce to a salad spinner and spin till as much water as possible is removed. Cover and store in the fridge until you are ready to assemble the salad.

When storing **mushrooms** always remove them from their plastic wrapping as this makes them sweat and they will go off faster.

Store **mussels** in salted water with oatmeal added to it in it in order to feed them and keep them alive. Discard any mussels that are open before you are ready to start cooking—they are dead. Likewise, discard any mussels that remain closed after cooking—they were dead before they were cooked.

Use a good vegetable **oil** for cooking—sunflower oil for frying and deep frying, and extra virgin olive oil for dressings. There's no point in using good, expensive olive oil for frying—you cook off most of the flavour.

When cooking **pulses** such as lentils, beans and peas, you should not add salt to the cooking water, as this prevents them from becoming soft and makes them indigestible.

Always store your **sea salt** in an earthenware or wooden container, as these natural materials absorb moisture and prevent dampness.

When cooking **spinach** all the liquid that is required is that which clings to the leaves after they have been washed.

Vegetables grown beneath the ground (potatoes etc.) should be cooked in cold water that is then brought to the boil while vegetables that are grown above the ground (broccoli etc.) should be plunged into rapidly boiling water.

Traditionally **whiskey** is never served with **oysters** as the combination is thought to cause stomach upsets.

I use packet **yeast** in my recipes—it's easily available and needs proving only once.

Part 1 Eating

1 Egg dishes

You can't really have a brunch party without an egg dish—firstly because they're traditional, secondly because they usually suit everybody, but mostly because they're cheap and very easy to cook.

Egg dishes for brunch take their origins from classical menus from far and wide, from breakfast dishes in their boiled, baked, poached or fried varieties to omelettes and soufflés as appetisers for both lunch and dinner. Eggs are popular all over the world.

When it comes to buying eggs, I recommend fresh farm eggs but fresh free-range eggs will do. Please don't buy any other kind as the life of a battery hen is pretty miserable and the eggs and chickens they produce are comparatively watery and tasteless. If you live in the country you will probably know somewhere to get fresh farm eggs and they really do taste better.

Eggs should be stored in the fridge or in a cool dark place. If you keep them in the fridge, you should take them out about an hour before cooking to allow them to come to room temperature. If eggs are boiled straight from the fridge, the shells will crack.

For brunch you should provide two eggs per person, but perhaps three in an omelette. As brunch is supposed to be a light meal and there are so many other great dishes in this book to serve with the eggs, that should be enough.

In the following pages I give you what I consider to be the easiest and most classically correct techniques for separating, whisking, poaching, boiling and scrambling eggs.

This is so that, as you work your way through the recipes, you can refer back to this section when you come to a particular technique.

How to separate eggs

Some recipes I have included require separated eggs. Here are two ways of doing this.

Break your egg open over a bowl and let the white pour over the edge of the shell into the bowl; then tip the yolk from one half of the shell to the other, until all the remaining albumen (egg white) has slid into the bowl.

Alternatively, make sure your hands are very clean, then crack the egg open and just pour it through your fingers over a bowl—the egg white will pour through, leaving you with an egg yolk in your hand ready to use. If there is some eggshell in your egg white, use another piece of eggshell to remove it.

How to whisk egg whites

When whisking egg whites you need to make sure your bowl and implements are completely spotless and totally grease free. A metal bowl is best. If you have one, a copper bowl actually reacts with the egg whites to make them thick and glossy.

Add a small pinch of salt to the egg whites—this helps the egg white to stiffen. Depending on the recipe, whip the egg whites until they form soft or stiff peaks.

How to poach eggs

The eggs you use for poaching should be really fresh so that the whites stay around the yolks; if they are not fresh the whites may disappear around the pan in strings.

Method

Bring a large, flat, wide pan of water to the boil and then turn it down to simmer.

Add a large drop of cider vinegar to the water. Stir the water rapidly before breaking the eggs into it as this helps the egg whites to keep their shape.

The eggs will take about 3½–4 minutes to poach until firm.

How to boil eggs

Actually boiling an egg is a mistake: ideally you should simmer them.

Bring a large pot of water to the boil and turn it down to a simmer. Add a drop of vinegar (cider is best) and add your eggs, preferably in a colander so they can easily be removed.

Simply simmer them for six minutes for soft boiled eggs or ten minutes for hard.

Poached eggs are delicious served with the following:

English muffins, avocado and tomato salsa (see page 49)

wild mushrooms, or asparagus, and hollandaise sauce (see page 36)

garlic croutons (see page 98)

How to scramble eggs

Simple scrambled eggs can be made even more delicious and different if you add various unusual ingredients to the basic recipe.

Method

Melt half the butter in a pot, preferably non-stick. Lightly beat the eggs. Add to the pot and stir continually over a low heat with a wooden spoon.

When the eggs have thickened slightly add the remaining butter, cut into cubes, the cream and salt and pepper to taste.

Just before the eggs are ready, take them off the heat. They will continue to cook from the heat of the pan.

Stir in the smoked salmon and dill, or other extras of your choice. Serve immediately.

Ingredients

2 oz/60 g/½ stick butter
2 eggs per person
1 tablespoon cream per person
salt
freshly ground black pepper

Optional extras

slivers of smoked salmon and
*   fresh dill*
freshly chopped herbs
fresh Parmesan shavings and
*   freshly ground black pepper*
fresh poached asparagus or
*   canned asparagus tips*
slivers of prosciuttio
slivers of foie gras
crumbled goat's cheese and
*   stoned, halved black olives*
Jalapeno chilli peppers with
*   grated Cheddar cheese,*
*   chopped scallions (green*
*   onions) and sour cream*

Eggs sur le plat

This is a good method for when you're cooking up a storm in the kitchen, you're using all your burners and you've got six guests hungrily waiting for brunch in your garden or dining room.

For this dish you will need a wide flat gratin dish or something similar.

Method

Preheat the oven to gas mark 5/190°C/375°F, or preheat the grill/broiler.

Lightly butter the dish and break your eggs into it. Season the eggs with salt and pepper and dot a few pieces of butter over the top.

Place the dish in the oven for about 10 minutes or grill (broil) gently until the eggs are how you want them.

Ingredients

1 oz/30 g/ ¼ stick butter per person
2 eggs per person
salt
freshly ground black pepper

Eggs en cocotte

Eggs en cocotte are eggs cooked in buttered ramekin dishes placed in a bain-marie (a baking tray half-filled with water) and then baked.

Method

Preheat the oven to gas mark 4/180°C/350°F. Butter the ramekins. Put a tablespoon of cream in the base of each ramekin and season to tase with salt and pepper.

(This is the time to add any optional extras such as mushrooms or tomatoes by placing a tablespoonful on top of the cream in each ramekin.)

Break an egg into each dish and dot each one with a little butter.

Place the dishes in a baking tray half filled with water, place in the oven and cook for about 20 minutes.

Serve in the individual dishes, decorated with fresh herbs.

Ingredients (for 4)

2 oz/60 g/ ½ stick butter
4 tablespoons cream
salt
freshly ground black pepper
4 large fresh farm eggs
fresh herbs to garnish

Optional extras

thinly sliced mushrooms
chopped tomatoes
crispy bacon pieces
cooked spinach
canned asparagus tips

Tortilla Espagnole—Spanish omelette

Serve this delicious omelette immediately, or make it the day before your brunch and serve it cold with bread as they do in Spain.

A neat trick for a party is to divide the mixture between cupcake tins and bake individual omelettes.

For this recipe you need waxy potatoes, for example new potatoes, washed, peeled and thinly sliced, preferably using a mandolin or food processor.

Method

Heat the olive oil in a large frying pan or skillet. Gently sweat the potato, onion and garlic for 12–15 minutes, until the onions are golden brown and nicely caramelised and the potato slices are just done.

Make sure the oil is not too hot or the garlic will burn and become bitter.

Beat the eggs with the seasoning and a little water.

To make one large omelette: add the eggs to the pan. Continue to cook on a low heat for a few minutes until the omelette sets. Try to ensure that it doesn't stick.

Ingredients (for 6)

2–3 tablespoons olive oil
6 medium potatoes, peeled and thinly sliced
2 Spanish onions, peeled and finely sliced
2 cloves garlic, peeled and finely sliced
6 eggs for one large omelette or 12 individual omelettes
sea salt, to taste
freshly ground black pepper, to taste

Brown the omelette under a low grill/broiler for a few minutes. Serve immediately or allow to go cold and serve the next day.

To make individual omelettes: divide the potato and onion mixture between 12 greased cupcake tins, pour the egg mixture on top and bake in the oven at a medium heat, gas mark 5/ 190°C/375°F until the omelettes are firm to the touch.

Garnish the little tortillas with finely-diced red pepper, sprigs of asparagus, slivers of smoked salmon or whatever inspires you.

Serve as above.

UFO eggs

I decided to try this simple recipe after seeing the movie, *Moonlighting*, where Nicholas Cage makes them for Cher after a stay-over. It's a delicious combination of fried bread and fried eggs. They're very bad for you but they look pretty and taste great!

I advise you to make this recipe in batches of twos or threes, wiping the pan clean with kitchen paper each time and starting with new oil and butter.

Method

Cut the bread into slices approximately 1 in/3 cm thick. Tear out the inside of the bread leaving about ½ in/2 cm all around. Heat a little oil in a non-stick frying pan and add a little butter. When the butter foams, add the bread to the pan until it is lightly coloured on the underside.

Crack your eggs into the centre of the bread slices and fry gently for a few more minutes. Very carefully turn over with a fish slice and cook until it's how you like it or how requested.

Serve UFO eggs with crispy bacon and the cocktail of your choice.

Ingredients (for 6)

1 Vienna loaf (not a baguette)
butter and oil for frying
6 eggs

Shirred eggs on toast

This dish is simple and elegant. It's very good served with a plain salad of mixed herbs for a healthy start to the day.

Method

Whisk the egg whites with a pinch of salt until they form soft peaks. Fold in half the cheese.

Spread the toast with the egg and cheese mixture leaving a dip in the centre.

Gently slide the egg yolks into the dip on each of the pieces of toast and sprinkle the remainder of the cheese over.

Cook under a medium grill/broiler until the egg whites are golden and the yolks are to your taste.

Serve garnished with the chopped herbs.

Ingredients (for 4)

2 egg whites
4 egg yolks
salt
2 tablespoons gruyère cheese, grated
4 pieces thick, crusty white bread, toasted
freshly ground black pepper
chives or parsley, chopped, to garnish

Eggs Benedict

There are a few things you should know about Eggs Benedict.

Firstly, hollandaise sauce is not impossibly difficult to make but it is a little bit tricky; however, it does keep for a while so you can make it before your friends arrive. If the sauce fails you can always try again without looking stupid.

Secondly, English muffins are used for the base but I find bagels pretty good or if you like you can use some good white bread.

Thirdly, you are supposed to use a circle of honey roast ham cut into the same shape as the English muffin, but your favourite grilled bacon will work just as well.

Method

Make the hollandaise sauce: boil the vinegar, water and 1 tablespoon of lemon juice in a small, heavy-based saucepan, until it is reduced to about one tablespoon. Add a drop of cold water to the reduction and transfer to a bowl.

Add the egg yolks and whisk until the mixture is smooth. Place the bowl over a pan of simmering water and whisk for a few moments, gradually adding the melted butter and whisking continuously.

Ingredients (for 4)

4 large fresh free range eggs, poached (see page 28)
4 slices cooked ham or 8 slices grilled bacon
2 English muffins

For the hollandaise sauce

1 tablespoon white wine vinegar
1 tablespoon water
1 ½ tablespoons lemon juice
2 egg yolks
6 oz/180 g/1 ½ sticks butter, melted
salt
freshly ground black pepper

If the mixture gets too hot the eggs will scramble so you should remove the bowl from the heat every so often and continue to whisk in the butter. It's easier if you get someone to hold the bowl while you whisk and pour.

The butter and eggs should emulsify and produce a delicious thick sauce which you should then season with salt and pepper and a little more lemon juice to taste.

Store in a warm place until ready to use, but not for more than an hour or so or it will curdle.

Now you have your hollandaise sauce ready, all you have to do is poach your eggs and assemble the dish.

Halve the muffins and toast them. Put them on your serving plates and cut the ham or bacon to sit nicely on the muffins.

Place the perfectly poached eggs on top, coat them with hollandaise and serve.

Baked eggs on mushrooms

The idea here is to construct a three-tiered breakfast. It's easier than it sounds and if you like you can place the whole lot on a round of toasted crusty bread. If you don't have any ramekin dishes simply skip the part about baked eggs. Poach or fry the eggs instead and place them on top of the tomatoes.

Method

Preheat the oven to gas mark 5/190°C/375°F.

Butter the inside of four small ramekin dishes and break an egg into each one. Place the dishes into a baking tray half filled with water and bake in the oven on a low heat until the whites of the egg are firm. This takes about 15 minutes.

Lightly fry the mushrooms in half the olive oil. Set aside and keep warm. Lightly fry the tomato slices in the remaining olive oil with salt and freshly ground black pepper. Poach or fry your eggs if you're not baking them.

Place the mushrooms on warmed plates. Place the slices of tomato on top of the mushrooms.

Turn the baked eggs out on top of the tomatoes, or place the poached or fried eggs on top. Garnish with fresh herbs and serve immediately.

Ingredients (for 4)

1 oz/30 g/ ¼ stick butter
4 eggs
4 large breakfast mushrooms, destalked
4 thick slices of beef tomato
1 tablespoon olive oil
salt
freshly ground black pepper
fresh herbs, for garnish

Piperade

From the Basque region of Spain, this is a mixture of scrambled eggs, peppers and tomatoes. It's very difficult to mess up as long as you don't overcook the eggs. Piperade is traditionally served with slices of sautéed Bayonne ham but you can substitute crisply grilled Irish streaky bacon or grilled pancetta if you wish.

Method

Heat the olive oil in a pan or skillet and cook the peppers and onion over a low heat for approximately 15 minutes.

Add the tomatoes, garlic, seasoning and basil. When the tomatoes are tender, add the eggs and stir continuously as for scrambled eggs.

When the eggs are nearly done take them off the heat and continue stirring as the heat from the vegetables will cook them a little more.

Stir in the basil and olives and serve immediately.

Ingredients (for 4)

2 tablespoons olive oil
2 green peppers, deseeded and
   sliced lengthways
2 red peppers, deseeded and
   sliced lengthways
1 small onion, peeled and sliced
1 lb tomatoes, roughly chopped
1 clove garlic, chopped roughly
salt
freshly ground black pepper
1 tablespoon fresh basil, torn
   roughly
4 large fresh farm eggs, lightly
   beaten
1 tablespoon black olives,
   stoned/pitted and roughly
   chopped

Spinach cocottes

This dish is a bit like a crude soufflé. It can be baked in four individual ovenproof dishes (cocottes or ramekins) a gratin dish or a small casserole dish. It's delicious with a salad and some herb mayonnaise made by simply adding the chopped herbs of your choice to mayonnaise.

Method

Defrost the spinach, drain thoroughly and chop finely.

Butter the ovenproof dish or dishes. Preheat the oven to gas mark 5/190°C/375°F.

With an electric whisk or hand blender, beat the eggs until they are frothy.

Fold in the cheese, spinach, breadcrumbs and, of course, salt and pepper.

Pour the mixture into the dish or divide it between the ramekins.

Bake in the oven for 20–30 minutes, or until golden brown.

Ingredients

8 oz/225 g/1 cup frozen spinach
butter to grease the oven dishes
3 eggs
3 oz/90 g/ ¼ cup extra mature
   Cheddar cheese, grated
3 oz/ 90 g/ ¼ cup breadcrumbs
salt
freshly cracked black pepper

Eggs baked in tomatoes

This is a really easy impressive recipe, delicious with home-made, or good shop-bought, brown soda bread and butter.

Method

Preheat the oven to gas mark 5/190°C/375°F.

Slice the tops off the tomatoes. Carefully remove and discard the inside pulp with a teaspoon or a parisienne spoon (melon baller) if you have one. Discard the pulp.

Break an egg into each tomato and sprinkle with salt and pepper. Replace the tops of the tomatoes.

Place the tomatoes on a lightly oiled baking tray. Bake in the oven for 10–12 minutes.

Ingredients (for 4)

4 large beef tomatoes
4 eggs
salt
freshly ground black pepper

2 Breads and pastries

There's nothing like the amazing aroma of freshly baked bread to welcome your guests.

Bread is the stuff of life, and making bread has to be one of the most satisfying things you can do; it has an almost primitive quality.

I've included a variety of different recipes, most of them are easy with some a little more tricky, but if you are so inclined, I urge you to give them a go.

If you are very busy and just don't have time to bake, good freshly baked bread is generally available. A good tip is to heat it briefly in the oven just before serving.

Baguette

Without doubt, it's far easier to buy freshly baked baguettes from your local shop than to make them yourself. However, if you follow this recipe carefully, you'll produce a really stunning crusty loaf just like the ones you get in France, with the bonus of the delicious smell permeating your kitchen.

The baguette gets its unique crust and texture from the steam applied during the first ten minutes of cooking, so this is an essential part of the recipe.

Method

Dissolve the sugar and yeast in the tepid water. Stir 10 oz/280 g/1¼ cups of the flour into the mixture but make sure it's not mixed in too thoroughly, as you need it to be lumpy. This mixture is called a ferment.

Cover the bowl with a tea towel and place somewhere warm for about an hour, or until the ferment doubles in volume.

Before it is ready, dissolve the salt in the warm water—not too hot, as too much heat would kill the yeast in the ferment.

Add the salt water to your ferment and mix in. The mixture will now look like a bubbling, floury mess, but persevere and

Ingredients (for 3 sticks)

½ teaspoon sugar
2 teaspoons dried yeast
8 fl oz/240 ml/1 cup tepid water
16 oz/450 g/2 cups strong white (unbleached all-purpose) flour
½ oz/15 g/1 tablespoon salt
2 fl oz/60 ml/¼ cup warm water

add the remaining flour. Mix it all together until it becomes recognisable as a dough and then turn it out onto a well floured board.

Knead the dough for just 2–3 minutes. Cover it with a damp tea towel and leave to stand for around 30 minutes at room teperature.

At this stage you need to preheat the oven to gas mark 8/450°F/230°C as it has to be very hot for this recipe. Place an empty clean roasting tin on the top shelf to heat it.

Divide the dough into three pieces and let them rest for five minutes before rolling out by hand into 10 in/25 cm batons. Score the batons diagonally with a sharp knife.

Take a clean dry tea towel and sprinkle it with flour. Place the rolls on it and cover with another tea towel. Let the rolls 'prove', or rise, for a final half hour.

Move the empty roasting tin to the bottom of the oven. Transfer the batons to a floured baking sheet and place on the top shelf of the oven.

Pour three-quarters of a cup of water into the empty roasting tin at the bottom of the oven. When you shut the oven door the oven will fill with steam.

After 10 minutes reduce the heat of the oven to gas mark 6/400°F/205°C and remove the water tray. Bake for a further 7–10 minutes.

Focaccia

This delicious Italian yeast bread is even better with sun-dried tomatoes, olives, cheese or fresh basil leaves sprinkled over it before cooking.

Method

Mix the table salt, yeast and flour in a bowl. Rub in 2 table-spoons of the olive oil. Add the water gradually; the mixture should be soft, but not too sticky.

Knead the dough well for about 10 minutes, until it is elastic and smooth. Put the dough into an oiled bowl and turn it over so it's coated with oil. Cover it with a tea towel and leave in a warm place to prove, or rise.

After about an hour it should have doubled in size. Give the dough a good wallop to knock the air out of it and knead it for a few more minutes. Roll it and stretch it to fit an oiled baking sheet.

Sprinkle the fresh rosemary leaves and the sea salt over the top and let the dough prove for another half hour.

Pre-heat your oven to gas mark 8/230°C/450°F.

Bake the focaccia for around 20 minutes until golden brown. Serve while still warm.

Ingredients

1 large pinch table salt

1 ¾ packets dried yeast (total ½ oz/15 g/1 tablespoon)

1 ½ lb/720 g/3 cups strong white (unbleached all-purpose) flour

3 tablespoons olive oil

12 fl oz/375 ml/1 ½ cups tepid water

2–3 sprigs fresh rosemary

1 teaspoon sea salt flakes

Yeast bread

In this recipe it is vital that you use strong (unbleached) flour to get the correct texture. If you use plain (all-purpose) flour, your bread will have the texture of a cake.

Method

Grease a large baking tray with vegetable oil.

Mix the dry ingredients together in a basin. Rub in the olive oil with your hands. Add the water, gradually mixing until you have a wet but firm dough.

Turn the dough out onto a well-floured surface and knead until it becomes smooth and silky. This should take 6–7 minutes.

Set the oven to gas mark 8/230°C/450°F.

Place the dough on the baking tray and cover with a plastic bag or tea-towel. Leave in a warm place for about 45 minutes or until the dough has doubled in size.

Bake the bread until it is golden-brown and hollow sounding when tapped on its base.

Ingredients

vegetable oil, for greasing
1 ½ lbs/720 g/3 cups strong white (unbleached all-purpose) flour
1 ½ packets dried yeast (just under ½ oz/15 g/1 tablespoon in total)
½ oz/15 g/1 tablespoon sugar
½ oz/15 g/1 tablespoon salt
4 fl oz/120 ml/½ cup olive oil
12 fl oz/360 ml/1 ½ cups luke-warm water

Flour tortillas

Very trendy flat Mexican peasant bread, easily available in most supermarkets, but check this out . . .

Serve with fried eggs, avocados and tomato salsa (see opposite) for traditional Mexican heuvos rancheros.

Method

Sift both the flours into a mixing bowl along with the salt.

Add the egg and water and mix with an ordinary table-knife. Draw the mixture together into a ball with your hands. At this stage, it should be neither sticky nor crumbly.

Knead the dough on a flat surface until it becomes smooth to the touch and doesn't crack. This should take about 5 minutes.

Divide the dough into 8 equal portions and then roll into balls. Cut 8 pieces of greaseproof/parchment paper into 6 in/15 cm diameter circles.

Roll each ball out between two pieces of the greaseproof paper. This is necessary for a smooth and even tortilla, but it does take a bit of energy.

Heat a large non-stick pan/skillet and remove the top sheet of paper from your tortilla.

Ingredients (for 8 tortillas)

4 oz/120 g/ ½ cup plain white
   (all-purpose) flour
4 oz/120 g/ ½ cup maize flour
½ teaspoon salt
1 egg
3 tablespoons water
oil for cooking—preferably
   corn oil

Brush the exposed side of the tortilla with a little oil and then place oiled side down onto the pan/skillet.

Peel off the second sheet of paper and cook the tortilla until the edges curl up slightly.

Turn with a spatula and cook on each side until golden-brown.

Remove from the pan and keep warm in tinfoil in a low oven until ready to serve.

Tomato salsa

Method

Squeeze the juice of the lime into a medium sized bowl.

Dissolve the sugar in the juice.

Toss the onion in the juice and set aside.

Cut the tomatoes in half, scrape out the pulp with a spoon and discard.

Chop the remainder of the tomato into small dice and add to the onion with the rest of the ingredients.

Mix well and serve with fried eggs and flour tortillas for heuvos rancheros.

Ingredients

1 lime
½ teaspoon sugar
½ red onion, peeled and finely diced
4 tomatoes
1 green chilli pepper, deseeded and finely diced
salt and pepper to taste
1 tablespoon coriander/ cilantro, roughly chopped

Brown soda bread

Brown soda bread made with wholemeal (wholewheat) flour is wholesome and nutritious and very easy to make.

Method

Grease and flour a baking sheet. Pre-heat the oven to gas mark 7/210°C/400°F.

Place the wholemeal (wholewheat) flour in a basin. Sift the rest of the dry ingredients together onto the flour in the basin.

Rub in the oil with your hands, add the milk and mix thoroughly. The dough should be quite wet, but still retain its shape.

Turn the dough out onto the baking sheet and make a cross with a large knife on the top of the loaf.

Bake for 45 minutes or until a knife blade comes out clean when inserted.

I find that a slightly damp cloth placed over the bread when removed from the oven produces a softer crust.

Ingredients

vegetable oil for greasing
1 ½ lbs/720 g/3 cups wholemeal (wholewheat) flour
¼ lb/120 g/½ cup self-raising white flour
½ teaspoon baking powder
½ teaspoon baking soda
1 tablespoon salt
2 fl oz/60 ml/¼ cup vegetable oil
1 pint/600 ml/2 ½ cups milk

White soda bread

White soda bread is soft and more like a cake than brown soda bread. It goes particularly well with home-made raspberry jam.

Method

Preheat the oven to gas mark 7/210°C/400°F. Grease and flour a baking sheet.

Place about three-quarters of the flour in a basin. Sieve the rest of the dry ingredients with the remaining flour into the basin.

Add the oil and rub in with your hands. Gradually add the milk and mix thoroughly. The dough should be wet but still retain its shape.

Turn the dough out onto the baking sheet and mark a cross on the top with a large knife.

Bake in the oven for 45 minutes or until a knife blade comes out clean when inserted.

Ingredients

vegetable oil for greasing
1½ lbs/720 g/3 cups self-raising
  white flour
½ tablespoon baking powder
½ tablespoon baking soda
2 fl oz/60 ml/¼ cup vegetable oil
1 pint/600 ml/2½ cups milk

Bagels

A traditional Jewish food, bagels have been wholeheartedly embraced all over the world. They go particularly well with smoked salmon and cream cheese or kippers and scrambled eggs. If you have a sweet tooth, black cherry preserve and sour cream with bagels make a great combination.

These 'breads' are not proved in the ordinary way but are dropped into boiling water briefly before being baked, giving them a dense texture and a glossy crisp crust. They take about 3 hours to make from start to finish.

Method

Grease a large baking sheet.

Sift the flour into a large basin.

Pour 4 fl oz/120 ml/½ cup of the water into a medium-sized pot with the salt, sugar and butter. Heat until the butter has melted, then allow to cool.

Take the rest of the warm water and sprinkle the yeast over it. Stir when it becomes frothy.

Whisk the egg white until it forms soft peaks and add to the flour in the basin with the liquids from the pot. Mix well and

Ingredients

vegetable oil for greasing

14 oz/420 g/1 ¾ cups strong white (unbleached all-purpose) flour

8 fl oz/240 ml/1 cup lukewarm water

1 teaspoon salt

2 tablespoons sugar

2 oz/60 g/½ stick butter

1 sachet dried yeast (½ table-spoon)

1 egg white

cover the basin with cling film.

Leave the mixture in a warm place until the dough has doubled in bulk, which should take around 2 hours.

Knock the dough back and knead for a few minutes, before cutting it into 1 oz/30 g/¼ stick pieces.

Roll each piece into a sausage shape about 6 in/15 cm long. Form each one into a ring by pinching the ends together. Leave to rest for about 15 minutes.

Meanwhile place a large pan of water on to boil and preheat the oven to gas mark 8/230°C/450°F.

Drop 3 or 4 bagels at a time into the boiling water and leave them until they rise to the surface. Place them immediately onto your baking sheet and then into the oven. Don't wait for all the bagels to boil before starting to bake.

After 10 minutes turn the bagels over and brush with a little beaten egg yolk.

Continue baking until they are golden brown.

Croisssants

Unless you really enjoy baking, are very good at it and have lots of spare time on your hands, you should buy croissants. However, if you want to give it a shot here's a good recipe. It will take up to 3 hours from start to finish.

Method

Oil a large plastic bag: drop in a teaspoon of oil, and then rub the bag to coat the inside with the oil.

Sift the flour, salt and sugar into a basin. Rub in 1 oz/30 g/¼ stick butter. Chop the remaining butter into small pieces, divide into three portions and place in the fridge.

Sprinkle the yeast over the lukewarm water and stir (it is important that the water is not too hot as this will kill the yeast). Stir the yeast liquid and the half of the beaten egg into the flour and mix.

Turn the dough out onto a floured board and knead until it is smooth and elastic, this will take at least 8 minutes. Place the dough in the oiled plastic bag and set aside for 15 minutes.

Roll out the dough into a rectangle of approximately 30 x 8 in/ 75 x 20 cm. Dot the top two-thirds of the dough with the little pieces of butter from the first portion.

Ingredients

vegetable oil for oiling
14 oz/420 g/1 ¾ cups strong
   (unbleached all-purpose)
   white flour
1 teaspoon salt
½ teaspoon sugar
7 oz/210 g/1 ¾ sticks butter
1 tablespoon dried yeast
7 fl oz/210 ml/¾ cup lukewarm
   water
2 eggs, beaten

Fold the bottom third of the dough up to the middle and the top third down over the first.

Pinch the edges together to seal in the butter and turn the dough 90° on the floured board. Roll out the dough, fold it in three again and give it a quarter turn again.

(At this stage you may want to put the dough in the oiled bag and place it in the fridge or deep freeze as it is easier to work with when chilled.)

Repeat the above steps twice to incorporate the remaining butter. Then chill the dough for a further 15 minutes.

Grease a large baking sheet. Roll the dough out into a rectangle of 14 x 9 in/35 x 25 cm and cut it into 6 squares. Cut these squares in half diagonally and brush with beaten egg.

Roll the wide edge of each triangle loosely towards the point, making sure the tip is underneath, and curve into a crescent shape.

Place the croissants on the baking sheet and place it in the polythene bag. Leave them at room temperature for about an hour to prove.

Preheat the oven to gas mark 7/220°C/425°F. Bake the croissants for 15–20 minutes or until golden brown.

Serve hot from the oven with butter and jam.

Danish pastries

Difficult but very tasty! I give instructions for two types, pinwheels and cartwheels. They are made from the same basic dough.

Method

Oil two large plastic bags: drop in a teaspoon of oil, and then rub the bags to coat the insides with the oil.

Melt 2 oz/60 g/¼ stick butter. Chop the remaining butter into small pieces, divide into three portions and place in the fridge.

Sift the flour, sugar and salt into a basin. Dissolve the yeast in the milk and add the melted butter. Add the milk mixture to the flour and mix it to a dough. Place in an oiled polythene bag and leave to rise at room temperature for an hour.

Punch down the dough and roll it into a rectangle of approximately 30 x 8 in/75 x 20 cm.

Dot the top two-thirds of the dough with little pieces of butter. Fold the bottom third of the dough up to the middle and the top third down over the first. Pinch the edges together to seal in the butter and turn the dough 90° on the floured board.

Roll out the dough, fold it in three again and give it a quarter turn again.

Ingredients

vegetable oil, for oiling
9 oz/270 g/2 sticks butter
12 oz/360 g/1 ½ cups plain white
   (all-purpose) flour
2 oz/60 g/ ¼ cup caster (super
   fine) sugar
¼ teaspoon salt
1 oz/30 g/2 tablespoons dried
   yeast
4 tablespoons warm milk
1 egg, beaten

For the pinwheels

2 oz/60 g/ ¼ cup apricot jam,
   melted
8 tablespoons marzipan

For the cartwheels

2 oz/60 g/ ½ stick butter
2 oz/60 g/ ¼ cup sugar
3 teaspoons cinnamon
2 oz/60 g/ ¼ cup sultanas (golden
   raisins)

(At this stage you may want to put the dough in one of the oiled bags and place it in the fridge or deep freeze, as it is easier to work with when it is chilled.)

Repeat the above steps twice to incorporate the remaining butter. Then chill the dough for a further 15 minutes.

Grease a large baking sheet. Divide your dough in two and roll it into rectangles measuring 16 x 8 in/40 x 20 cm.

Make the pinwheels: cut one rectangle into 8 squares. Brush the squares with the jam.

Place a tablespoon of marzipan in the centre of each square. Make a cut from the corners of each square to the centre. Press every second point into the centre of the square to achieve a pinwheel effect.

Place the pinwheels onto a greased baking tray, brush with beaten egg and place inside one of the oiled bags. Leave to rise in a warm place for 15 minutes.

Make the cartwheels: place the butter, sugar and cinnamon in a bowl and mix together.

Spread the butter mixture evenly over the remaining rectangle of dough. Sprinkle liberally with sultanas/golden raisins and roll up from one end.

Cut the roll into 8 slices and place them on a greased baking sheet. Squash them down a little, brush with beaten egg and place in the second oiled bag. Leave to rise in a warm place for about 15 minutes.

Preheat the oven to gas mark 7/220°C/425°F. Remove the plastic bags and bake the pastries for 15–20 minutes or until golden brown.

Brioche

A mixer or food processor will help for this classic. If you haven't got a brioche tin a loaf tin will do. Be prepared to spend up to 2 hours making brioche.

Method

Lightly oil a large basin.

Grease the brioche or loaf tin. Sprinkle the yeast over the milk and let it stand.

In the bowl of your mixer or processor, place the eggs, butter, sugar, salt, lemon zest and yeast mixture. Mix well and gradually add the flour. Let it mix until the dough becomes smooth.

Place the dough in the oiled basin. Cover and leave it to rise in a warm place until the dough has doubled in bulk, which should take around 40 minutes.

Punch the dough to release the air and place it in your loaf or brioche tin, pressing it in hard. Cover with a tea towel and leave to rise for about 25 minutes, or until it doubles in size.

Preheat your oven to gas mark 5/375°F/190°C.

Brush a little beaten egg or milk over the brioche and bake for 40–45 minutes.

Ingredients

vegetable oil
1 tablespoon dried yeast
4 fl oz/120 ml/½ cup warm milk
5 eggs, beaten
6 oz/180 g/1 ½ sticks butter
1 ½ tablespoons sugar
½ teaspoon salt
1 lemon, grated zest of
8 oz/240 g/2 ½ cups plain white
  (all-purpose) flour

Beignets

Beignets are deep-fried pastries, dusted with icing sugar and served with *café au lait* in the Deep South of the USA. They taste a bit like doughnuts and are remarkably similar to the Spanish churro which is another deep-fried pastry, piped through a star nozzle into boiling oil and dredged with castor sugar and cinnamon before being served with cups of obscenely thick hot chocolate.

It's a good idea to have plenty of kitchen paper to hand to drain the beignets before serving.

Method

Sieve the flour into the bowl. Put the water, butter and salt in a pan and bring to the boil. Add the flour and remove the pan from the heat, stirring to make a smooth paste that doesn't stick to the sides of the pot.

Allow it to cool slightly before adding the egg yolk, beating well to incorporate it. Add the whole eggs one at a time beating until the paste is shiny.

Heat the oil over a medium heat until very hot, in other words about 360°F or 185°C.

If making beignets, drop tablespoonfuls of paste into the oil.

Ingredients

4 oz/120 g/ ½ cup plain white (all-purpose) flour
8 fl oz/240 ml /1 cup water
2 oz/60 g/ ½ stick butter
pinch of salt
2 eggs
1 egg yolk
3 pints/2 litres/ 6 cups sunflower oil for deep-fat frying
1 tablespoon caster (super fine) sugar

If you want to make churros, put the paste into a piping bag with a star nozzle which measures ½ in/1 cm and pipe 3 in/5 cm lengths directly into the oil. They will naturally form twists.

Cook the fritters in the oil until they are crisp and golden, then drain on kitchen paper before dredging in sugar.

Blinis

These are a must with caviar, and they are also delicious with crème fraîche and black cherry preserve for those with a sweet tooth. It's worth going to the trouble of making blinis, as you cannot buy decent ready-made ones anywhere.

Method

Sprinkle the yeast into half of the warm water and milk mixture. Place the buckwheat flour in a basin, add the yeast mixture and stir well. Cover with a damp cloth and set aside to rise in a warm place.

Sieve the plain flour with a pinch of salt into another bowl. Add the egg, egg yolk, butter and remaining milk and water and mix well. Add the first batter and mix well. Cover again with a damp cloth and leave to rise for about 2 hours.

Before cooking whisk the egg white to stiff peak (that's stiffer than soft peaks) and fold into the batter. Heat a small non-stick pan over a medium heat and melt a little butter in it.

Drop about 2 tablespoons of the mixture onto the pan and cook. Turn the blini when bubbles rise on the surface.

Serve hot with caviar (or lumpfish caviar or salmon roe) and sour cream.

Ingredients

1 tablespoon dried yeast
½ pint/300 ml/1 ¼ cups mixed
    warm milk and water
4 oz/120 g/ ½ cup buckwheat
    flour
4 oz/120 g/ ½ cup plain white
    (all-purpose) flour
1 egg, beaten
1 egg yolk, beaten
1 tablespoon melted butter
1 egg white
pinch salt

3 Seafood

Oysters

A few oysters go a long way in the glamour stakes at a brunch party, although they can be expensive and difficult to open.

Overall, the most important thing I can say about oysters is that they *must* be fresh, and should not be opened in advance.

Basically they should either be eaten raw and alive or they should be cooked. If they are alive the shells will be tight shut. If the shell is even slightly open, and does not close when you knock it, throw it away. Shellfish poisoning is horrible.

The simplest and most elegant way of serving this fantastic aphrodisiac is raw and in the shells, served on ice garnished with seaweed and accompanied with wedges of lemon, Tabasco sauce and freshly-made brown soda bread.

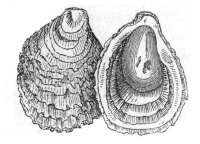

How to open oysters

The easiest way to open oysters is—to get someone else to do it. However, if you don't have an expert to hand, this is how to do it.

You need a sturdy short-handled knife, preferably an actual oyster knife (like the one below). If you are really stuck, you can use a large flat-bladed screwdriver, but be careful.

Wrap your hand in a tea towel—this prevents injury if the knife slips—hold the oyster firmly and place it on a work surface with the deep shell side down.

Push the tip of the knife into the crevice at the hinge of the oyster and force it in, then twist the blade. This is quite difficult until you get the hang of it.

Slide the blade along the roof of the oyster, cutting the muscle, and remove the top shell.

Run the blade under the oyster and flip it over, trying not to lose any of the delicious juice. Pick out any bits of shell that may have come loose.

Iced shellfish platter

To make a really *good* iced shellfish platter all you need is a really good fishmonger (and a deep pocket). The fish must be fresh and well cooked, and if your fishmonger cooks fresh fish all you have to do is buy it. If you're doing the cooking yourself, follow the instructions on pages 66-7.

Lobsters and crabs should be cooked from live. I'm sorry but I can't get sentimental about them, I look at lobsters and crabs as large delicious sea insects. If you chuck them into boiling water they die really fast. If you can't bear to kill them you can buy them cooked.

You can be as economical or as generous as you wish because this dish is suitable as both an appetiser and an entrée. The presentation of the dish is important: it should be quite dramatic, so buy lots of ice and assorted citrus fruit.

Place the ice on one or several large platters. Arrange the shellfish on the ice and garnish with wedges of the citrus fruit and some flat-leaf parsley.

Serve with lots of fresh brown bread, freshly ground black pepper, Tabasco sauce and home-made mayonnaise (see page 78).

Ingredients

Choose from the following:
lobster
crab
prawns
mussels
scallops
winkles
oysters

For garnish

limes
lemons
ice
flat-leaf parsley

How to cook lobsters and crabs

Bring a large pot of salted water to the boil. Add three table-spoons of vinegar.

Plunge in the lobster or crab and cover with a lid. Bring to the boil and allow to simmer for ten minutes.

Take off the heat and let the seafood cool in the cooking water.

How to prepare lobster meat for serving

Cut off the claws and pincers and crack them with the back of a large heavy knife.

Insert the knife into the top of the tail on the underside and cut down the centre firmly. Turn the lobster over and cut down the centre of the carapace (waistcoat).

Remove the stomach sac and the gills and the black trail that is the intestine. Everything else is edible.

How to prepare crab meat for serving

Cut off the claws and pincers and crack with the back of a heavy knife. Turn the crab on its back and remove the soft undershell .

Remove the gills and the sac behind the eyes and everything else is edible.

How to cook prawns

Bring a large pot of salted water to the boil and add a table-spoon of vinegar. Throw in the prawns and cook rapidly for 2 to 3 minutes.

Drain and rinse under cold water.

How to cook periwinkles

Bring a pot of salted water to the boil and add the winkles.

Bring the water back to the boil for 1 minute and then drain.

Rinse the winkles under cold water.

You will need to provide ordinary straight pins for your guests to pick the winkles out of their shells.

How to cook mussels

Scrub the mussels in cold water and throw away any that are open or damaged.

Place the mussels in a pot with a glass of white wine and cover with a tight fitting lid.

Cook over a high heat until all the mussels have opened. Throw away any that remain closed as these are dead.

Cockles and clams can be cooked in the same way as mussels.

Oysters Rockefeller

I don't know where this recipe comes from—presumably the USA— but I do know that it's very easy and delicious.

Method

Preheat your grill/broiler.

Melt the butter in a saucepan. Gently sauté the onion and garlic for about 1 minute. Add the spinach and cook until it has wilted, about 2 minutes. Season with black pepper.

Place the opened oysters on a heatproof dish. Place the spinach on top of the oysters. Sprinkle with the Parmesan shavings and place under the hot grill/broiler until the Parmesan has coloured slightly.

Traditionally, these oysters are served on a bed of rock salt but I have no idea why—maybe to balance the oyster shells and stop them from rocking on the plate.

Ingredients (for 4)

2 tablespoons butter
1 onion, peeled and finely sliced
1 clove garlic, peeled and crushed
½ lb/240 g/1 cup washed baby spinach
freshly ground black pepper
12 opened oysters
1 tablespoon fresh Parmesan shavings
rock salt

Cajun prawns

The beauty of this recipe is that it takes hardly any preparation and it's very delicious.

Cajun flavouring is a fiery mixture of peppers and spices used in the cuisine of the American Deep South where the concept of brunch originated. These spices are easily available from most supermarkets.

The only equipment you need is a baking tray and some tinfoil. If you're having quite a few guests to brunch it's worth buying large boxes of frozen tiger prawns from an Asian supermarket.

Method

Preheat your oven to gas mark 7/220°C/425°F.

Rinse the prawns and place them in a large roasting tin. Sprinkle them liberally with the Cajun spices. Pour over the wine and the melted butter and cover with tin foil.

Place in the oven for about 10 minutes or until the prawns are bright pink and firm to the touch.

Serve with freshly baked baguette (see page 44), and provide fingerbowls and plenty of napkins.

Ingredients (for 4)

20 large raw unshelled tiger
    prawns
1 tablespoon Cajun spices
¼ bottle dry white wine
¼ lb/120 g/1 stick butter, melted

Crab cakes

I have a passion for these and they are really easy to make. Crab meat is expensive but you can pad the mixture out with mashed potato or a cooked flaked fish such as cod or haddock. You are limited only by your imagination.

Method

Squeeze the crab meat to remove excess liquid and place it in a large basin.

Add the peppers, onion, egg, mayonnaise, lime, coriander and seasonings and mix thoroughly.

Add the breadcrumbs gradually until you have the right consistency to easily shape the mixture into small cakes. These shouldn't be too dry or else they'll break up when you start to cook them.

Heat some oil on a large frying pan. Fry the crab cakes until they are brown on either side. This will take about 10 minutes.

These are particularly good with chilli mayonnaise, which is made by adding about 1 teaspoon of chilli sauce to 8 fl oz/240 ml/1 cup mayonnaise.

Ingredients (for 16 small cakes)

1 lb/480 g/2 cups crab meat, picked over to remove all the small pieces of shell
½ red pepper, cut into very small dice
½ green pepper, cut into very small dice
½ red onion, cut into very small dice,
1 medium egg
2 tablespoons mayonnaise
1 lime, juice and grated rind of
1 tablespoon fresh coriander (cilantro) leaves, chopped
salt
freshly ground black pepper
3 oz/90 g/¾ cup soft fresh white breadcrumbs (to bind the mixture)
2 tablespoons sunflower oil for frying

Kedgeree

A traditional Anglo-Indian breakfast dish, kedgeree is very tasty and can be part prepared in advance. It's best to cook the rice on the day.

Method

Heat the oil and butter in a large pan. As the butter foams, add the onion, garlic and ginger and cook until transparent.

Add the curry powder and cook for a little longer, stirring continuously.

Add the cream and heat through.

If you are part preparing in advance you could let this mixture cool and refrigerate it until you are ready to complete the dish. Then proceed as follows.

Cook the rice and mix it thoroughly with the curry and cream mixture. Add the flaked fish and the boiled eggs.

Place in a serving dish, sprinkle with the parsley and serve hot.

If it needs reheating beause you have part prepared it, dot the surface of the kedgeree with butter, cover with tinfoil and place in the oven at gas mark 4/180°C/350°F for about 30 minutes.

Ingredients (for 6)

2 tablespoons olive oil
1 tablespoon butter
1 onion, peeled and diced
2 cloves garlic, peeled and crushed
1 tablespoon fresh ginger, peeled and chopped
1 tablespoon medium curry powder
5 fl oz/130 ml/¾ cup cream
6 oz/180 g/¾ cup basmati rice
1½ lb/720 g/3 cups smoked haddock, poached, drained and flaked
2 hard-boiled eggs, quartered
2 tablespoons parsley, roughly chopped

Lobster Newburg

I chose this classic because although it sounds complicated, it's actually very simple to prepare. Also, it uses cooked lobster which you can buy if you're squeamish or don't feel like battling with a prehistoric-looking live lobster on a Sunday morning.

Method

Prepare the lobster meat: remove the meat from the shell and cut it into chunks.

Melt the butter in a large heavy-based pan. Sauté the lobster meat in the butter for 2–3 minutes.

Add the brandy and sherry and cook for a further minute—don't worry if it goes on fire, the flames will die down quickly but just in case have a damp cloth at the ready.

Add the cream and reduce slightly. Gradually add the beaten egg yolks and seasonings.

Serve on hot toast, garnished with shavings of fresh parmesan and some sprigs of flat leaf parsley. For a dramatic effect, you could add a further garnish of a piece of lobster shell such as the tail or head.

Ingredients (for 4)

2 cooked lobsters
2 oz/60 g/ ½ stick butter
3 teaspoons brandy
3 teaspoons dry sherry
½ pint/300 ml/1 ¼ cups cream
4 egg yolks, lightly beaten
cayenne pepper to taste
salt to taste

To serve

thick crusty bread, toasted
Parmesan cheese
flat leaf parsley

Lobster, green bean and new potato salad

This salad looks great if arranged nicely on individual plain plates. It is extremely simple to make because it uses cooked lobster, so all you have to do is cook the beans and the potatoes. Preparing a live lobster can be quite a daunting task, and isn't really necessary.

The secret to the salad is to dress the potatoes while they're still warm. This makes all the difference.

Method

Cook the green beans in boiling salted water until they are just done, in other words still with a bite. Drain. Refresh the beans in cold water, drain and put aside.

Simmer the potatoes in salted water until just done. Drain and cut in half lengthways.

Make the dressing: place the oil, shallot, vinegar, salt and pepper in a bowl and mix thoroughly. Toss the potatoes in this mixture and allow to marinate for a few minutes.

To serve: remove the potatoes from the bowl and arrange on individual plates. Arrange the cooked lobster on top of the potatoes. Toss the beans in the remaining dressing in the bowl and scatter over the salad. Garnish with herbs and the remainder of the dressing.

Ingredients

1 small or ½ large cooked lobster per person
10 green beans per person
1 lb/480 g/2 cups new potatoes, washed and scrubbed
1 shallot, peeled and finely chopped
5 ½ tablespoons good olive oil
2 tablespoons white wine vinegar
sea salt
freshly ground black pepper to taste
fresh herbs to garnish

Potted shrimps

It's really worth investing in enough ramekin dishes to make individual portions of this dish. They're not very expensive and, as all good cooks know, presentation is half the battle when entertaining. It's best to make potted shrimp a day in advance.

Method

Melt two-thirds of the butter in a pan and gently sauté the shrimps.

Add the spices and seasoning and cook until the shrimps are firm and turn from an unhealthy-looking grey to an appetising pink.

Divide the shrimps equally between the ramekins and pour a little of the cooking butter over each. Allow to cool.

Melt the rest of the butter and pour over the shrimps to seal them.

Place a garnish of fresh herbs on top of each ramekin and chill in the fridge until ready.

Serve with fresh crusty bread or hot toast.

Ingredients (for 4)

3 oz/90 g/ ¾ stick butter (no
    substitute will do)
12 oz/360 g/ ½ cup raw shrimps,
    peeled
¼ teaspoon nutmeg
pinch powdered cloves
freshly ground black pepper
fresh herbs, to garnish

Fish cakes and Mayonnaise

Fish cakes are essentially comfort food, but are also really good for entertaining large numbers, as you can make the mixture up and chill it in the fridge overnight.

Method

Cook the potatoes in a pot of boiling, salted water until they are tender. Drain thoroughly and mash, mixing in the butter and milk. Add the fish, herbs, pepper and salt and set aside to cool.

Stir in the beaten egg yolk and, if the mixture seems too wet, add some flour. Divide the mixture into eight and shape into cakes.

Place the remainder of the flour in a bowl and season with the cayenne pepper, black pepper and salt.

Heat the oil in a shallow pan. Coat the fishcakes well in the flour and fry for around 4 minutes on each side, or until they are golden brown and crisp.

Serve with mayonnaise (see page 76) and a salad or with one of the egg dishes from Chapter 1.

Ingredients

1 lb/480 g/2 cups potatoes, peeled
1 oz/30 g/2 tablespoons butter
2 tablespoons milk
12 oz/360 g/1 ¼ cups white fish, cooked and flaked
1 tablespoon parsley, chopped
1 teaspoon dill, chopped
salt
freshly ground black pepper
1 egg yolk, beaten
3 oz/90 g/ ½ cup plain white (all-purpose) flour
vegetable oil for frying
pinch cayenne pepper

Mayonnaise

Most people think that making mayonnaise is beyond them but this is not so. You can make this recipe in a liquidiser or with an electric whisk, but when making a small amount I prefer to use a bowl and a hand whisk.

Substituting balsamic vinegar for white wine vinegar gives the mayonnaise a lovely sweetness.

One thing to be careful of is to keep the mayonnaise well refrigerated before serving, and not to let dishes that include mayonnaise get warm, in sunlight, for example.

It's also important to make sure that all your ingredients are at room temperature as this will help to prevent curdling.

Plain mayonnaise is a really good accompaniment to seafood or salads but it can be livened up with the addition of herbs, garlic or even chilli sauce. These additions work perfectly well, and indeed will improve, shop-bought mayonnaise.

Method

Place the bowl on a damp cloth as this will keep it stable when you are mixing.

Place the egg yolks in the bowl with the vinegar, mustard and salt and beat them a little with a whisk.

Continue to beat the mixture and add the oil drip by drip. The mixture should begin to thicken.

Continue adding the oil gradually, whisking constantly until all the oil is incorporated.

At this stage the mayonnaise should be thick and glossy. Now taste it to see if it needs more salt or vinegar.

If you wish, add the herbs, garlic or chilli sauce, tasting to check the flavour is how you like it.

Ingredients

2 egg yolks
1 tablespoon white wine or
    balsamic vinegar
1 teaspoon English mustard
pinch of salt
8 fl oz/240 ml/1 cup oil (use
    sunflower oil for a light
    mayonnaise or olive oil for a
    heavier sauce)

Optional extras

finely chopped herbs
puréed, roasted garlic
chilli sauce

Smoked salmon hash

Another very easy recipe. It's a simple mixture of tasty ingredients and it doesn't have to turn out in a perfect shape. A non-stick pan (skillet) will help.

Method

Boil the potatoes in salted water until they are just done. Place in a mixing bowl.

Sauté the peppers and onion in the butter and add to the potatoes. Add the salmon, cream, herbs, lemon zest and seasoning and mix lightly.

Heat two tablespoons of oil in a non-stick frying pan/skillet over a medium heat. Add the mixture to the pan//skillet and press down to make an even, compact cake.

Cook over a low heat for 10–15 minutes until a crusty base is formed. Place a large plate over the pan/skillet and turn it upside down so the cake turns out onto it.

Heat a little more oil in the pan/skillet and slide the cake back on so that the uncooked side is face down, and cook for a further 10 minutes.

Turn out onto a plate. Cut into wedges and garnish with sour

Ingredients (for 4)

1 lb/480 g/2 cups potatoes, peeled and diced
1 green pepper, seeded and diced
1 small onion, peeled and diced
1 oz/30 g/2 tablespoons butter
14 oz/420 g/1 ¾ cups smoked salmon, cut into strips
3 fl oz/90 ml/½ cup cream
2 tablespoons fresh mixed dill, parsley and chives, chopped
2 tablespoons lemon zest
freshly ground black pepper
sunflower oil for frying

To serve

Sour cream or crème fraîche

cream or crème fraîche

If, per chance, your hash refuses to form into a perfect cake simply tower it up in the centre of the plate and garnish with a sprig of dill or a few chives.

For extra decadence, try serving the hash with a poached egg sitting on top.

Kippers with creamed horseradish sauce

Kippers are split herrings dipped in brine (salt water), dried and then cold-smoked over beech or oak chips.

Method

Cook the kippers by standing them for five minutes in a jug filled with hot water.

You can now grill them if you wish.

Mix the horseradish with the vinegar, salt and pepper to taste.

Fold in the cream and sprinkle with the chives.

You can, of course, always just add whipped cream to bought horseradish sauce and garnish with chives to get a similar effect.

Ingredients (for 4)

4 kippers
3 tablespoons fresh horseradish root, peeled and finely grated
1 tablespoon white wine vinegar
salt
freshly ground black pepper
4 oz/120 g/ ½ cup cream, whipped
1 small bunch chives, finely chopped, or snipped with scissors

4 Savoury Things

Croque Monsieur

The classic French baked or fried sandwich is quite easy to make. I give two versions here. It's important to use gruyère cheese for both versions as it imparts a specific flavour.

If you place a poached egg on top of Version 1 you can call it a Croque Madame.

Version 2 is particularly comforting when your head is thumping in that oh-so-special way.

For this variation, you put the buttered side of the bread on the outside of the sandwich and fill it with ham only, as the cheese goes in the sauce instead.

Method for Croque Monsieur 1

Remove the crusts from the bread and make 4 sandwiches with the ham and cheese.

Heat the oil in a large frying pan or skillet. Fry the sandwiches over a medium heat until both sides are golden brown.

Dead easy!

Method for Croque Monsieur 2

Remove the crusts from the bread and make the sandwiches, buttered side outside.

Make the sauce: melt the butter in a pot over a low heat. Add the flour and cook for 2–3 minutes, stirring continuously.

Add the milk very gradually, stirring all the time to ensure that lumps don't form. If lumps do form, take the sauce off the heat and briefly blend with a hand blender.

Add the salt, pepper and cheese and continue to cook for a further 1–2 minutes.

Spread the sauce on top of the sandwiches and bake in a low oven for 10 minutes or until the sauce is golden.

Ingredients (for 4)

8 slices white bread, buttered
4 slices thinly cut lean ham
4 slices gruyère cheese
vegetable oil for frying

Ingredients (for 4)

8 slices white bread, buttered
4 thin slices lean ham

For the gruyère cheese sauce

2 oz/60 g/ ¼ stick butter
2 oz/60 g/ ¼ cup plain white
  (all-purpose) flour
1 pint/600 ml/2 ½ cups milk
salt
freshly ground black pepper
4 oz/120 g/ ½ cup gruyère
  cheese, grated

Sweetcorn fritters

These are very good with a spicy tomato salsa (see page 49) served with heuvos rancheros or with crisply grilled bacon and maple syrup.

Method

Place all the ingredients, except the flour and oil, in a bowl and mix.

Add the flour and mix or beat to make a batter thick enough to drop off a spoon.

Pour oil to a depth of about 1½ in/3 cm into a heavy pan (skillet). Heat over a medium heat until gently smoking.

Spoon the mixture into the hot oil one teaspoon at a time and fry until golden brown. If the fritters are too large or the oil is too hot, they will be raw in the centre and burnt on the outside, so keep the oil at a medium heat.

Remove the fritters from the oil and drain on kitchen paper.

Ingredients (for 4)

7 oz/210 g/¾ cup sweetcorn off
   the cob
1 large egg
2 scallions (green onions),
   finely chopped
2 teaspoons medium curry
   powder
1 teaspoon cayenne pepper
½ teaspoon salt
3 oz/90 g/¼ cup self-raising white
   flour
corn oil for frying

Pork sausages

I guarantee you will be very pleased with yourself indeed when you make this recipe.

You will need sausage casings—I get mine from isaac, my local butcher with attitude, but I'm sure any good quality butcher in your area would oblige. If not, you can make the sausage mixture into a log shape, wrap it in clingfilm, chill it, slice it and fry it.

It is very important to keep the pork at a low temperature as the blades in your blender may actually heat it up. If you freeze it before processing it will be easier to cut evenly.

Method

Spread the pork dice out on a tray and place in the deep freeze until almost frozen.

Put the pork in your food processor and process with regular blades until coarsely ground.

Crush the remaining ingredients with a pestle and mortar and mix well with the pork.

At this stage fry a teaspoon of the mixture, taste and adjust the seasoning accordingly.

Ingredients

1 lb/480 g/2 cups pork belly, cut
   into 1 in/2 cm dice
1 clove garlic, crushed
1 teaspoon dried sage
1 teaspoon salt
½ teaspoon of freshly ground
   black pepper
½ teaspoon of dried thyme
¼ teaspoon of cayenne pepper
¼ teaspoon of ground allspice
sausage casings

To stuff the sausage casings: take a manageable length of sausage casing and run water through it to clean it and open it.

Tie a knot in one end and pull the open end over the spout of a funnel you have previously cleaned.

Slide the casing onto the spout of the funnel until you reach the knot.

Work the filling through the funnel into the casings as you feed the casings out, but be sure not to fill it too much or the sausages may burst while being cooked.

Twist the sausages approximately every 4 in/6 cm. If you're making cocktail sausages twist them every 2 in/3 cm.

Refrigerate overnight before cooking in the usual manner.

Chorizo sausages

This is a Spanish sausage flavoured with garlic and paprika. It is usually air-dried or smoked and then served cold in slices. The version given here is fresh and needs to be cooked before serving.

Method

Spread the pork dice out on a tray and leave in the deep freeze until almost frozen.

Put the pork in your food processor and process using regular blades until it is coarsely ground. Add the back fat cubes to the pork.

Add the garlic, wine, spices and salt and mix together thoroughly.

At this stage, fry a teaspoon of the mixture, taste it and adjust the seasoning accordingly.

To stuff the sausage casings: take a manageable length of sausage casing and run water through it to clean it and open it.

Tie a knot in one end and pull the open end over the spout of a funnel you have previously cleaned.

Slide the casing onto the spout of the funnel until you reach the knot.

Ingredients

1 ½ lbs/720 g/3 cups pork belly, cut into 1 in/2 cm dice
¼ lb/120 g/½ cup pork back fat, without rind, in ¼ in/½ cm cubes
3 cloves garlic, peeled and crushed
2 fl oz/60 ml/¼ cup red wine
10 oz/300 g/1 ¼ cups sweet paprika
1 teaspoon crushed dried red chillies
½ teaspoon ground coriander/ cilantro
½ teaspoon ground cumin
¼ teaspoon freshly ground black pepper
1 teaspoon salt
sausage casings

Work the filling through the funnel into the casings as you feed the casings out, but be sure not to fill it too much or the sausages may burst while being cooked.

Twist the sausages approximately every 4 in/6 cm.

Refrigerate overnight before cooking in the usual manner.

Black pudding and apple hash

This is an Irish version of an American classic, using black pudding in place of corned beef. It's extremely easy to make because it's a simple mixture of tasty ingredients and doesn't rely on exact presentation to look good. You will find a non-stick pan (skillet) helps.

Method

Boil the potatoes in salted water until they are just done. Place in a mixing bowl.

Melt the butter and sauté the pepper, onion and apple. Add to the potatoes.

Heat a little oil and sauté the black pudding for 2 minutes. Add to the potato mixture. Add the herbs, mustard and seasoning and mix lightly.

Heat two tablespoons of oil in a non-stick frying pan/skillet over a medium heat. Add the mixture to the pan and press down to make an even, compact cake.

Cook over a low heat for about 10–15 minutes until a crusty base is formed.

Place a large plate over the pan and turn it upside down so the

Ingredients (for 4)

1 lb/450 g/2 cups potatoes, peeled and diced
1 oz/30g/ ¼ stick butter
1 green pepper, diced
1 small onion, peeled and diced
1 apple peeled, cored and diced
sunflower oil for frying
14 oz/420g/1 ¾ cups black pudding, peeled and cut into cubes
2 tablespoons fresh herbs, eg thyme and parsley, chopped
1 teaspoon English mustard
salt, to taste
freshly ground black pepper, to taste
sour cream, crème fraîche or mayonnaise, to garnish

cake turns out onto it.

Heat a little more oil in the pan and slide the cake back on so that the uncooked side is face down, and cook for a further 10 minutes.

Turn out onto a plate and serve in wedges garnished with sour cream, crème fraîche or mayonnaise.

If your hash refuses to form into a perfect cake simply tower it up in the centre of the plate and garnish with a couple of chives.

For extra indulgence, try serving this with a poached egg sitting on top.

Devilled kidneys

Not for the squeamish, but a very tasty traditional brunch dish that costs very little.

Method

Melt the butter in a small pan and gently cook the onion until transparent.

Add the kidneys and cook gently in the butter.

Mix the rest of the ingredients in, adding the brandy last.

Cover the pan and simmer for about fifteen minutes.

Serve with fresh baguette or brown soda bread.

Ingredients (for 4)

2 tablespoons butter
1 onion, finely diced
8 lambs' or calves' kidneys,
   peeled, halved and cored
½ teaspoon salt
½ teaspoon cayenne pepper
1 teaspoon Worcester sauce
2 tablespoons fresh lemon juice
½ teaspoon English mustard
3 tablespoons brandy

Welsh rarebit

An overlooked comforting classic. The topping can be made in advance and stored in the fridge.

Method

Melt the butter in a saucepan, add the flour and cook, stirring constantly.

Blend in the milk and then the beer. Add the mustard, Worcester sauce and seasoning.

Add the cheese gradually while stirring constantly.

At this stage you can cool the mixture and store it in the fridge until you are ready to serve the rarebit.

To serve simply spread the mixture on toast and place under a hot grill or broiler until the mixture bubbles.

Ingredients

1 oz/30 g/ ¼ stick butter
1 tablespoon plain white/all-purpose flour
2 tablespoons milk
3 tablespoons beer, preferably ale
1 teaspoon English mustard
Worcester sauce, to taste
6 oz/180 g/ ¾ cup Cheddar cheese, grated
salt, to taste
pepper, to taste

Creamed mushrooms on toast

This is another very easy brunch dish suitable for vegetarians. You can use any variety of mushrooms—whatever's available.

Method

Quarter the mushrooms and sauté lightly in three-quarters of the butter.

Melt the remaining butter in a pan and add the flour. Cook gently.

Add the cream gradually and stir continuously until you have a smooth sauce.

Add the sauce to the mushrooms and season with the salt, pepper and cayenne.

Serve on hot toast.

Ingredients

½ lb/240 g/1 cup mushrooms
4 oz/120 g/1 stick butter
1 ½ tablespoons plain white/all-
  purpose flour
8 fl oz/240 ml/1 cup cream
salt
freshly ground black pepper
cayenne pepper, to taste

Liver in cream and stout sauce

You can use either calves' liver or lambs' liver for this dish. It's very good with potato farls (see page 94) or fried bread. Any brand of stout or dark ale will do.

Method

Preheat the oven to very low.

Heat the oil and butter in a pan until it is barely smoking. Add the liver and onion.

Cook the liver briefly on both sides then remove from the pan to a low oven to keep warm. (It's important not to overcook liver as it will get tough.)

Reduce the heat under the pan and cook the onions for about 5 minutes more until they are soft.

Add the stout, pinenuts and herbs and let the liquid reduce slightly.

Stir in the cream, taste the sauce and season accordingly. Return the liver to the pan and heat through.

Serve like Tournedos Rossini: on fried bread with the sauce poured over.

Ingredients

1 tablespoon vegetable oil
1 teaspoon butter
1 lb/480g/2 cups calves' or lambs' liver, thickly sliced
2 onions, peeled and sliced thinly
5 fl oz/150 ml/¾ cup stout or dark ale
2 tablespoons pinenuts
2 tablespoons parsley and thyme, chopped
8 fl oz/240 ml/1 cup cream
salt
freshly ground black pepper

Potato farls

A traditional Irish potato bread which is very good served with fried bacon, sausages and eggs.

Method

Boil, drain and peel the potatoes. Mash the potatoes with the salt and butter. Cool.

Work the flour in to the mash to make a dough. Knead lightly on a floured surface. Roll out until it is about ¼ in/1 cm thick. Cut into triangles.

Cook on a hot greased griddle or pan (skillet) until golden brown on both sides. Serve hot with butter.

Ingredients

1 lb/480 g/2 cups old, as opposed to new, potatoes
1 teaspoon salt
1 oz/30 g/¼ stick butter
3 oz/90 g/½ cup plain white/all-purpose flour
vegetable oil, for greasing
butter, for serving

Hash browns

A traditional, delicious, American brunch potato dish. The genuine article—a world away from the processed, deep-fried potato flour nugget things we get on the Irish side of the Atlantic.

Method

Cook the potatoes until they are half done. This should take about 15 minutes. Drain and let them cool until they are comfortable to handle.

Peel the potatoes and grate roughly into a bowl. Add the onion. Season with salt and pepper.

Heat the oil and butter in a large pan (skillet); when hot, add the potato. Press it into the pan in a cake shape—do not stir.

Cook over a low heat for about 10 minutes. The potatoes should form a crust on the base.

Invert the cake onto a plate and add a little more oil to the pan. Allow the fat to heat and slide the cake back onto the pan for a further 10 minutes to cook the other side.

Turn out onto a heated plate and serve in wedges.

Serve with sour cream and salsa.

Ingredients

*1 potato per person
¼ onion, finely diced, per person
salt
freshly ground black pepper
butter for frying
vegetable oil for frying*

Potato latkes

Forget the fashionable potato rosti, these traditional Jewish potato cakes are much more delicious and even easier to make. Traditionally, they are made with Matzo meal and fried in Schmaltz (rendered chicken fat) but I have modified this recipe to make it more supermarket-friendly.

Method

Grate the potatoes into iced water; this prevents them from going black.

Squeeze the potatoes dry between your hands and place in a mixing bowl.

Add the rest of the ingredients, except the oil and butter, and mix well.

Heat a little oil in a pan and add a knob of butter. When the butter sizzles, drop spoonfuls of the mixture into the pan to form small flat cakes.

Brown the latkes on both sides.

Serve with crème fraîche and caviar.

Ingredients

6 medium potatoes, peeled
1 onion, peeled and grated
2 eggs, beaten
3 tablespoons plain white (all-purpose) flour
salt
freshly ground black pepper
vegetable oil for frying
butter for frying

Cheeseboard

A good cheeseboard looks impressive, is convenient and pleases pretty much everybody. Irish farmhouse cheese is excellent and is widely available at supermarket cheese counters and from specialist shops.

Buy a couple of whole good cheeses or freshly cut *large* pieces as these look and taste far more attractive than a lot of scrappy little pieces of cheese.

When in a supermarket ask the person behind the counter what's good and if they answer with any sort of enthusiasm go with their suggestion. However, if you are limited to pre-packaged cheese a good general rule is that the nearer the expiry date the nicer it will be.

Keeping cheese in the fridge isn't recommended as it will dry out. It should be kept in a cool, dry place. A larder or pantry would be ideal; otherwise keep the cheese in a biscuit tin, in your garage or garden shed, or on your balcony. If you have a soft or blue cheese that smells strongly it's probably best to keep it in its wax paper and then wrap it in tin foil.

Always let cheese come to room temperature before serving as this brings out its true flavours. Serve cheese very simply by just presenting it on a large board with seasonal fruit and accompanied by fresh crusty bread or crackers.

Garlic croutons

Delicious with poached eggs, or in hot or cold soups, or sprinkled on salads.

Method

Preheat the oven to gas mark 4/180°C/350°F.

Put the garlic in a pot and cover it with the oil.

Place over a low heat and cook gently until the garlic colours. It's important not to let the garlic burn.

Take the oil off the heat and put it aside to cool.

Place the oil in a bowl with the salt and toss the bread cubes in it so that they are lightly coated.

Spread the bread evenly on a baking tray and bake in the oven for half an hour, turning every ten minutes.

Ingredients

10 slices white bread, cut into
   small cubes
2 cloves garlic, peeled and
   sliced thinly
4 tablespoons olive oil
pinch of salt

5 Sweet and Fruity Things

French toast—pain perdu

The French name for French toast translates literally as 'lost bread'. This refers to yesterday's bread rescued and made edible by being dipped in a mixture of egg and milk and then browned in butter.

A fine way of jazzing this up is to make a fruit- or preserve-filled sandwich and then dip it in the egg mixture before frying. You can replace half the milk in this recipe with cream for an even richer, calorie-laden brunch.

Method

Mix the egg, milk, sugar, vanilla and cinnamon in a wide dish.

Dip the slices of bread or sandwiches into the mixture, making sure that they are thoroughly coated.

Melt the butter in a pan (skillet) and when it is foaming fry the bread on both sides until golden brown.

Ingredients (for 4)

2 eggs, beaten
6 fl oz/180 ml/¾ cup milk (or cream)
1 tablespoon sugar
½ teaspoon vanilla essence or preferably the pulp from a vanilla bean
½ teaspoon cinnamon
4 slices of bread, or 4 sandwiches
butter for frying

Honey oven-pancake

This pancake is suitable for a number of people and is handy if you are using all the burners on the cooker.

Method

Place the butter in a 10 in/15 cm oven-proof dish—you could use a quiche dish, or even a frying pan with a heatproof handle or individual ramekin dishes.

Place the dish or dishes in the oven as it is preheating to gas mark/425°F/°C. Remove from the oven when the butter has melted.

While the butter is melting beat the eggs until light and frothy. Gradually add the honey and milk. Bit by bit, add the flour and salt, beating until the batter is smooth.

Pour the batter into the dish of hot butter and return to the oven.

Bake for about 20 minutes or until golden brown and puffed and the blade of a knife comes out clean when inserted. (If you're making a number of smaller pancakes the cooking time will be shorter.)

Cut into wedges and serve with seasonal fruit and crème fraîche or sprinkled with castor sugar and fresh lemon juice.

Ingredients (for 6)

4 oz/100 g/ ½ stick butter
3 eggs
3 tablespoons honey
3 oz/90 g/6 tablespoons plain
   white/all-purpose flour
¼ teaspoon of salt
14 fl oz/420 ml/1 ¾ cups milk

Banana hot cakes

When developing this recipe, I had intended to see if they would freeze but they didn't survive long enough in my kitchen to make it to the freezer . . .

Method

Place the flour, baking powder, salt, nutmeg and sugar into a basin.

In a separate large bowl beat the egg and milk together with the vegetable oil. Add the bananas and the lemon juice.

Add in the flour mixture and stir lightly until combined—it should be a little lumpy.

Heat a little oil in a non-stick frying pan and pour about 3 tablespoons of batter onto it.

Cook over a low heat until the cakes are puffed and golden brown. Turn and repeat until all the batter has been used up.

Keep the cakes warm in a low over until ready to serve.

Ingredients (for 10 cakes)

4 oz/120 g/ ½ cup plain white (all-purpose) flour
2 teaspoons baking powder
½ teaspoon salt
⅛ teaspoon nutmeg
2 tablespoons sugar
1 egg
4 tablespoons milk
3 tablespoons vegetable oil
2 bananas, mashed
2 teaspoons lemon juice
sunflower oil for frying

Chocolate and walnut muffins

There will be no danger that you will opt for the commercial kind after you have discovered how easy it is to make these amazing things. Seriously.

Method

Preheat the oven to gas mark 7/400°F/220°C. Grease a muffin tin or have paper cases ready.

Sift the flour, sugar, cocoa, baking powder, bread soda, cinnamon and salt into a basin.

Mix together the eggs, milk and melted butter and add to the dry mix. Stir lightly to mix and then fold in the nuts.

At this stage, if you wish, you can add in a chopped-up bar of your favourite chocolate.

Fill the muffin cases threequarters full and bake in the oven for approximately 15 minutes or until the blade of a knife comes out clean when inserted.

Ingredients (for 12 muffins)

7 oz/210 g/1 cup white plain
   (all-purpose) flour
3 oz/90 g/6 tablespoons sugar
6 tablespoons cocoa powder
2 teaspoons baking powder
½ teaspoon baking soda
2 teaspoons cinnamon
¼ teaspoon salt
2 eggs, beaten
4 tablespoons milk
4 oz/120 g/1 stick butter,
   melted
2 oz/60 g/ ¼ cup walnuts,
   coarsely crushed

Bircher muesli

This recipe is so good for you that a small portion of it will make you feel positively virtuous before you start eating fried food and quaffing champagne cocktails. It also tastes fabulous.

Method

Toast the oats on a dry tray in a low oven for about 15 minutes and cool.

Toast the walnuts in the same oven for about 8 minutes and cool.

Place the oats in a basin and add the milk, yoghurt and apricots. Cover and refrigerate overnight.

Before serving, add the nuts and grapes to the bowl.

Halve and core the apples and grate them directly onto the mixture.

Mix well and serve in bowls with extra milk and honey to taste.

Ingredients (for 4)

2 oz/60 g/ ¼ cup rolled oats
2 oz/60 g/ ¼ cup walnuts, coarsely chopped
4 fl oz/120 ml/ ½ cup milk
6 oz/180 g/ ¾ cup plain yoghurt
3 oz/90 g/6 tablespoons dried apricots, coarsely chopped
2 green apples
5 oz/150 g/10 tablespoons seedless grapes, halved

Iced fruit platter

Fruit salads are refreshingly elegant and simple. I emphatically recommend them as part of your brunch menu, served with home-made yoghurt (see page 108). Here is one of my favourite ways of serving fresh fruit.

Method

Take a large serving plate and arrange segments of a variety of the freshest, best looking fruit you can find.

I'm giving you a selection of fruit divided into different colour categories so you can easily choose a tricolour effect or a dramatic single colour effect. As usual, imagination is the scarce resource . . .

If using bananas, toss the slices in lemon juice to stop them discolouring.

Just before serving sprinkle the platter with ice cubes.

Red fruits
strawberries
cherries
black grapes
raspberries
red apples
redcurrants
fresh figs
water melons
pomegranate seeds

Green fruits
kiwi fruit
green apples
green melon
green grapes
limes

Orange and yellow fruits
oranges
peaches
pineapples
bananas
papaya
mangoes
kumquats
nectarines
clementines

Sparkling melon

Another of my favourite ways of serving fresh fruit. This dish is made with the use of a parisienne spoon which is popularly known as a melon baller. Now widely available in supermarkets, it's dead easy to use.

Method

Make balls of melon with the parisienne spoon or neatly cut the melon into cubes and refrigerate.

In a serving bowl, mix together the balls of melon with the lemon juice and nutmeg.

Just before serving, pour over the Asti or the cider.

Ingredients (for 4)

1 honeydew melon
1 cantaloupe melon
2 teaspoons lemon juice
¼ teaspoon freshly grated nutmeg
1 cup Asti spumante
  or sparkling cider

Pineapple and banana kebabs

For a totally tropical taste!

Method

Turn on your grill or broiler. Mix together the lime juice and the honey.

Cut the pineapple and bananas into large chunks of a similar size.

Thread the chunks onto skewers and brush them with the lime juice mixture.

Place the skewers under the hot grill (broiler) and turn at regular intervals until they caramelise.

Serve with the ice-cream of your choice, coconut if available.

Ingredients (for 4)

1 lime, juice of
1 teaspoon honey
1 fresh pineapple, peeled and cored
3 large bananas

Home-made yoghurt

Delicious with fresh fruit.

Method

Scour and rinse a large bowl with boiling water and set aside.

Heat the milk until it has just boiled then remove from the heat immediately.

Cool until the milk is hand hot, i.e. just above lukewarm. Stir in the yoghurt.

Pour into the bowl that you have sterilised and cover very securely with clingfilm.

Wrap the bowl up in towels, as this helps maintain the temperature that the bacteria needs to work. Place the bowl in a warm place overnight (the hot press/airing cupboard for example). Alternatively you can pour the mixture into a wide-necked thermos flask.

In the morning either whisk the mixture or pour off the whey (the liquid) if you prefer your yoghurt more solid. Chill in the fridge until it is needed .

Serve with fresh fruit, fruit compote or honey and hazelnuts.

Ingredients

16 fl oz/480 ml /2 cups
  skimmed milk
4 fl oz/120 ml /½ cup Greek
  yoghurt

Grilled pink grapefruit

This is a particularly easy starter for a 1970s style brunch party.

Method

Heat your grill.

Cut the grapefruit in half and run a sharp knife around the edge between the flesh and the pith. Run the knife between the segments also.

Mix some sugar and cinnamon together and sprinkle liberally over the surface of the fruit.

Place the grapefruits on a baking tray and place under the grill or broiler until the sugar bubbles.

Serve hot and sweet.

Ingredients

½ juicy pink grapefruit per person
caster (super fine) sugar, to taste
ground cinnamon, to taste

Cinnamon toast

An old favourite, and rightly so. It is particularly good when made with brioche.

Method

Preheat your grill or boiler. Lightly toast the bread on each side.

Mix the butter with the sugar and add cinnamon to taste.

Spread the toast with the cinnamon mix and grill (broil) until the sugar bubbles.

Serve hot.

Ingredients

2 thick slices of white bread or brioche per person
1 oz/30 g/ ¼ stick butter per person
1 teaspoon sugar per person
ground cinnamon, to taste

Lemon curd

Excellent on croissants or indeed any of the breads in this book. You'll need some clean jam- or other jars. Put a metal spoon into each jar before pouring in the hot lemon curd to prevent the glass from cracking. Then remove the spoon.

Method

Put a pot of water on to simmer.

Place the sugar, butter, lemon zest and juice into a bowl and sit it on top of the pot of simmering water. Stir until the sugar has dissolved.

Remove from the heat and add the eggs. Return the bowl to the heat and stir constantly until the mixture thickens.

It is important not to let it boil or it will separate.

Pour the curd into the clean jars and let cool.

The curd will keep in the fridge for up to two weeks.

Ingredients

8 oz/240 g/1 cup sugar
3 oz/90 g/¾ stick butter
2 lemons, zest and juice of
3 eggs, beaten

Part 2 Drinking

6 Drinks to make you feel Good

Fruit juices

The days are long gone when fruit juice meant sticky condensed stuff out of a can; these days most people are aware of just how good a freshly squeezed juice can be.

Most health-conscious cafés will have their own juicer, and there are few things as fine as freshly squeezed apple juice made with fresh apples.

Also, don't be afraid to combine juices into non-alcoholic cocktails.

Here's one of my particularly favourite recipes that can be made without a special juicer:

Fresh fruit shake

This is great, and would be ideal ammunition before the onslaught of a brunch party . . .

Method

Place all the ingredients into a blender and whizz for around 30 seconds.

The drink will look like a banana milkshake but it's much better for you.

Here are a few other combinations that work well together:

fresh apple and cranberry juice

fresh rasberry and orange juice

melon and kiwi fruit

Ingredients

1 pint/600 ml/2 ½ cups freshly squeezed orange juice
2 bananas, peeled and halved
2 kiwi fruit, peeled
1 crisp eating apple, peeled and cored

Coffee

For really good coffee, you need to buy coffee beans and grind them fresh. However, if you can't or won't do this, then be sure to buy a really good brand of ground coffee.

If you are only having a few for brunch and have a cappuccino or espresso machine, that's great but I find for entertaining and convenience, a cafetière (plunger jug) is best.

A good tip for a better taste is to heat milk in a pot and whisk it with a hand mixer before pouring into hot fresh coffee. This can do wonders for an inferior coffee; even instant coffee can be raised above its usual level by making it with hot whisked milk.

An indulgent variation is mocha coffee, made with stror espresso, a couple of spoonfuls of good chocolate powder milk and crowned with whipped cream.

A drop of almond-flavoured Ameretto liqueur will enric coffee.

Tea

You can't really beat Irish breakfast tea, but the wonderfully scented Earl Grey is lovely for a treat.

If you are not from Ireland, this is how you make tea.

Fill the kettle with freshly drawn cold water and boil.

Warm the pot by filling it with boiling water and leaving it for a minute before emptying.

Put 1 teaspoon of tea per person in the pot. Fill with boiling water and let stand for 3 minutes. Pour through a tea strainer into china cups.

Milk, lemon and honey should be passed at the table to taste.

Iced tea

Iced tea's full name is St Louis Iced Tea, after the place of its invention, the 1904 St Louis World Fair.

Method

Strain the hot tea and add the lemon rind and honey or sugar.

Stir to dissolve the sugar or honey and allow to cool. Remove the rind.

Place plenty of crushed ice in four glasses, along with the slices of lemon. Pour the tea over the ice.

Garnish with mint and lounge by your pool.

Ingredients

1 pot freshly-made tea
2 strips lemon rind
caster (super fine) sugar or
*   honey to taste*
4 lemon slices
4 sprigs mint

7 Drinks to make you feel Better

Champagne

Well, what can I say? 'Yes!', usually.

It's the perfect brunch drink and, indeed, brunch is the perfect excuse to drink champagne. If it's a really special occasion, a very expensive champagne well chilled will go well with just about everything.

If it's just for the hell of it, a champagne cocktail made with a good cava or a non-vintage champagne is more than acceptable.

A good idea for chilling champage if you are entertaining on a grand scale and the fridge is full, is to half-fill your bath with cold water and throw in a couple of bags of ice. This creates a giant ice-bucket.

Champagne cocktail

This is truly a delicious drink.

Place a sugar cube in each glass, add a drop of Angostura Bitters and a teaspoon of brandy.

Top the glass up slowly with champagne and serve.

Bellini

A classic cocktail, originating in Harry's Bar in Venice and bloody good on a Sunday morning.

Peel the peaches and remove the stones.

Place in a blender with sugar and lemon juice and process until smooth.

Strain into a bowl and refrigerate (this can be done ahead of time).

Half fill champagne glasses and stir in a tablespoon of peach mix.

Top up with champagne and serve.

Ingredients

1 sugar cube
1 drop Angostura Bitters
1 teaspoon brandy
nv champagne

Ingredients

peach, ½ per glass
sugar, to taste
lemon juice, to taste
nv champagne

Mimosa

Much more sophisticated than Buck's Fizz.

Pour an inch of orange juice into each glass and add a teaspoon of liqueur.

Top up with champagne, stir and serve.

Ingredients

¼ cup freshly squeezed orange
   juice, per glass
1 teaspoon orange-flavoured
   liqueur
nv champagne, chilled

Bloody Mary

How to make a bloody good bloody Mary . . .

If you are making this for a brunch party it is a good idea to multiply the measures and make a load of it in a large jug.

Take a tall glass and place three or four cubes of ice in it.

Combine all the ingredients together to your own taste and pour over the ice.

It's important not to add the ice unless it is going to be consumed immediately because (God forbid) the ice might melt and dilute the perfect drink.

Ingredients

1 large shot cold vodka
½ fresh lemon, juice of
1 dash cold dry sherry
tomato juice, to taste
Worcester sauce
Tabasco sauce
celery salt
freshly ground black pepper

Harvey Wallbanger

Pour the vodka and orange juice over ice in a tall glass.

Float the Galliano on top.

Drink.

Ingredients

¼ cup vodka
½ cup fresh orange juice
1 ½ teaspoons Galliano

Tequila Sunrise

Pour the tequila and orange juice over ice in a tall glass.

Add the grenadine last so it sinks to the bottom leaving a 'sunrise' in your glass.

Ingredients

¼ cup tequila
6 tablespoons orange juice
2 teaspoons Grenadine

Margherita

Rub a segment of the lime around the rim of your glasses, and dip in a saucer of salt to give a frosted edge.

Put 2 teaspoons of lime juice, the tequila and triple sec in to a cocktail shaker with ice.

Shake well and then strain into your glasses.

Ingredients

1 lime, segment and juice of
salt for frosting glasses
2 tablespoons tequila,
1 tablespoon orange flavoured
    liqueur

Red eye

This is a traditional hangover cure—if you can keep it down, you're cured!

Pour both ingredients into a tall glass at the same time. Try to drink it.

Ingredients

½ cup lager
½ cup tomato juice

Pina colada

Blend the ingredients with ice until smooth.

Pour into half a coconut and garnish with strawberries, cherries, umbrellas and sparklers. Lovely Jubbly.

Ingredients

¼ cup Bacardi
2 tablespoons coconut cream
   (available in tins)
½ cup pineapple juice
coconut shells, for serving
strawberries, cherries etc for
   garnishes

Iced Baileys coffee

Make the coffee or espresso and set aside to cool.

Shake the coffee, milk and Baileys together in a cocktail shaker and pour into tall glasses over ice.

Top off with a spoonful of whipped cream and sprinkle with a teaspoon of chocolate.

Ingredients

1 shot espresso or very strong coffee
1 cup milk
1 shot Baileys
ice
1 tablespoon whipped cream
1 teaspoon grated chocolate

Oyster shooter

Beloved of my good friend Sara Burke.

Put the oysters into a shot glass

Add the half-shot of vodka.

Season to taste with lemon juice, Tabasco sauce, salt and pepper.

Phwooarr . . .

Ingredients

2 oysters
½ shot frozen vodka
lemon juice
Tabasco sauce
salt
pepper

INDEX